T0145203

Nacho's New Home

Cassandra Anandappa

To order additional copies of this book, contact:
Xlibris
844-714-8691
www.Xlibris.com
Orders@Xlibris.com

ISBN: Softcover   978-1-6698-0695-0
         EBook   978-1-6698-0694-3

Print information available on the last page

Rev. date: 01/15/2022

NACHO'S NEW HOME

Written and Illustrated by
Cassandra Anandappa

Nacho and his sister Chubbie were cats, and they needed a home. They were tired of their little cage in the pet store. It was hard to find a forever home - no one seemed to want *two* cats. But Nacho and Chubbie could not - and would not - be separated.

Then one day, a Man with a Beard and a Long-haired lady noticed them. They bent down to peer into their cage, smiling warmly. They held Nacho and Chubbie a while, snuggling and nuzzling them, petting them gently. It had been a long time since the cats had been cuddled. Nacho was not sure if he liked it.

The Man with the Beard and the Long-haired Lady said, "We are going to take you home and love you forever!"

"What is love?" Nacho asked Chubbie.

"I don't know," she replied, "but we will find out!"

So Nacho and his little sister Chubbie rode home with the Man with the Beard and the Long-haired lady in their car. It was a bumpy, noisy ride, but at long last, they made it to their new home.

Chubbie seemed so happy, and so did the Man with the Beard and the Long-haired Lady. But Nacho was not so sure. This place was much bigger than their little cage in the pet store.

There were lots of climbing places....

and lots of hiding spaces.

The cats even had their own little house, with toys that jingled and crinkled and squeaked when they pounced on them!

Chubbie liked when the Man with the Beard and the Long-haired Lady picked her up. She purred and purred, rubbing her head into their chests.

The Man with the Beard and the Long-haired lady held Nacho, too. They petted him and scratched behind his ears.

But Nacho always tried to wiggle away. He didn't purr, and he pulled his head away from their hands. He preferred to stay far away on his windowsill.

While Nacho was resting on his windowsill, the Man with the Beard and the Long-haired lady petted him, but Nacho would yell, "Meow!" and scratch them with his claws!

The Man with the Beard looked mad, and the Long-haired Lady looked sad.

The Man with the Beard and the Long-
haired Lady still petted him,
and they still fed him,
and they still snuggled with him.

One day, Nacho tried to climb a shelf, and he knocked over a picture frame. It fell to the floor with a crash!

The Long-haired lady cleaned up the mess, and Nacho thought she would be angry.

The Long-haired Lady picked up Nacho and held him close.

"You silly cat," she said, smiling. "Don't worry, I can always replace that old frame." She kissed him on the nose. All was forgiven!

The next evening, Nacho smelled something tasty! He followed his nose into the kitchen...

and found a yummy piece of fish!

He quickly gobbled it up, but the Man with the Beard walked in and caught him!

At first he looked mad, but then he shook his head and laughed.

"Sorry, buddy, I guess we should have fed you sooner! Good thing we made plenty more fish for dinner!" And all was forgiven!

The next day, while the Man with the Beard and the Long-haired Lady were out of the house, Nacho went exploring.

He found a big wooden box sitting in a sunny spot on the floor, and inside the box was a turtle!

"Hello, Mister Turtle, I'm Nacho, what is your name?" said Nacho.

"My name is Jack," said the turtle. "It's nice to finally meet you, I could hear you stomping around out there!"

"How long have you lived here, Jack?" asked the cat.

"I have lived with the Long-haired Lady for sixteen years," said Jack, smiling proudly. "I have lived with her since she was just a little girl. She has moved many places, but she always took me with her, and now here we are

"Wow! That is a long time! Can you tell me... do you know what love is?"

"Of course I do!" said Jack, happily. "It's all around us."

"How do you know?" said Nacho.

"Our humans show us love, because they want us to be happy. They feed us, they give us a safe place to live, they hug us, and pet us, and talk to us.

"Most of all, they are kind to us, even when we bite them, scratch them, or break their things by mistake."

"My sister and I had humans before the Man with the Beard and the Long-Haired Lady found us," said Nacho sadly. "Those humans got angry when we broke things, and made us sad. Then they gave us away.

"Those humans were mean, so these ones must be mean, too." Nacho looked very sad.

"Are these humans mean to you here?" said Jack.

Nacho thought for a moment. "No, I guess not. They are kind to us, even when we don't behave."

Jack smiled warmly. "That, Nacho, is love."

"But what good is love? What do you do with it?" Nacho was so confused.

"You see, Nacho, love is like an ocean. It is deep, and wide...

"and you can give away buckets and buckets of it.

"But just like the rain fills the oceans again, those who receive love can shower others with it...

"and those who gave away all those buckets of water will still have so much left over!"

"So, our humans will love us forever?" Nacho felt a warmth in his chest rise up and spread, and he felt himself rattling in his belly - he was purring! He felt happy for the first time in a very long time.

Later that day, when the Man with the Beard and the Long-haired Lady came home, Chubbie and Nacho ran to them and jumped in their arms, much to their humans' surprise!

Nacho purred and licked the Man's face. The Man with the Beard laughed and said, "Oh Nacho, I love you too."

As Nacho rubbed his head against the man's beard, the Man with the Beard hugged him tighter.

From that day on, Nacho behaved himself. He did this even when his humans were busy... even when his humans seemed mad...

and even when his humans made mistakes.

He only climbed on his house instead of up the drapes or on the wooden furniture.

He ate only the food in his bowl instead of stealing food from the table.

He played nicely with his sister Chubbie and his new brother Jack, and he purred and purred as he cuddled with his humans when they let him sit on the couch.

"We love you, Nacho," said the Man with the Beard and the Long-haired Lady. "Meow!" Nacho said out loud, but what he was really saying was, "I love you too!"

THE END

Printed in the United States
by Baker & Taylor Publisher Services